Sugar and Spice

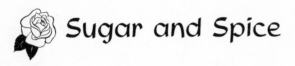

Illustrated by Jack Phillips

Designed by Paul S. Zell

SUGAR and SPICE

by
Elinor K. Rose

THE FIVE OAKS PRESS

Royal Oak, Michigan

The author is grateful to the editors and publishers of
*Christian Herald, McCall's, Reader's Digest, The Saturday
Evening Post* and *The Wall Street Journal* for permission
to reprint some of these verses. Most of them originally
appeared in the syndicated daily newspaper features *Life-
lines, Out Woodward Way, Rosettes* and *Sugar and Spice.*

To my husband
Dana
and our three sons
Stuart, Douglas, Bruce

We have three boys we try to raise,
Each has his own distinctive ways;
But truly, I'll be more than glad
If they grow up to match their Dad!

Foreword

Light verse, at its best, is more than gay, charming or light-hearted. It also gives off light, illuminating some phase of human experience with witty wisdom. No one else, the reader notes happily, has ever said it quite that way before.

That is how it is with the verses of Elinor K. Rose. Disciplined to the rigid framework of quatrain or couplet, they are more than merely clever. The last line, the last phrase, often the last word, flashes incandescence. The periodic expression, even more difficult to bring off in verse than in prose, is her specialty.

Her sharp perception and her technical skill with the ultimate thought are two reasons that the reader's "favorite" verse by Mrs. Rose is likely to be the one he is reading.

W. Sprague Holden

Chairman, Department of Journalism
Wayne State University

Contents

Home Is Where the Mortgage Is

FANCY SEEING YOU HERE

The house looks messy, so do I;
The doorbell peals an urgent cry.
"Drop in sometime" I often say,
But gad, I didn't mean today!

PRIVATE DOMAIN

Home is your castle, a place within which
You always are able to scratch when you itch.

HOUR SHOWER

In a family of six a bathroom is where
Somebody else is already there.

SCAT SYMPHONY

Romances of cats inevitably flower
To a musical score that's incredibly sour.

BOOM OR BUST

To market, to market, my pocketbook fat;
Home again, home again, utterly flat.

RELATIVELY SPEAKING

When visited by kith and kin,
   He tires of them forthwith;
It's not the kin that do him in
   But all their little kith.

I WANT AN ESCALATOR CLAUSE

When I depart this life I fear
The elevators, same as here,
Will pass me with indifferent frown;
I'll ring for up, they'll all go down.

ROVER

He doesn't consider himself a pet
He's sure he's one of the family yet;
What happens inside his little brain-cogs?
Does he think he's people or think we're dogs?

'TWAS EVER THUS

How much our children seem to know!
   We're glad they're so well-versed.
In fact, we'd like to tell them so
   Except they tell us first.

JUST LI'L OLE ME

I like potato chips and cokes,
I giggle at the oldest jokes;
I may be dumb, I may be plain,
But what a snap to entertain!

FOOT-IN-MOUTH DISEASE

I did it again
  With my usual skill;
I opened my trap
  When I should've kept still.

EARLY DAZE

Here by the laundry chute I stand
Three dirty kitchen towels in hand;
Someway my plans got snafued up,
What's down the chute? My coffee cup.

SN-NAP!

Our house won't go to bed at night
It yawns and stretches out of spite;
Why can't it wait to creak and creep
Until I'm decently asleep?

LOUD PLAY RECORDS

Our friends like stereophonic sound;
And when we visit them I've found
The background music played could be
A little farther back for me.

SOMETHING INNATE

There comes a moment in everyone's life,
However deft with a fork and knife,
Whether a blue-blood or only a twerp—
When a body'll burp.

WARNING MUTTER

For hours I've soothed each small complaint,
I've smiled as patient as a saint;
But now my halo's turning brittle
And Mama's gonna snarl a little.

POOR TIMING

If I were a watch
    With wheels for a mind,
I still would be running
    Five minutes behind.

IT'S A DRAW

Their mantel wall is blank and bare.
    "A painting," she insists, "Or nothing."
    "Some antique guns," he says, "Or nothing."
So nothing's what they've got up there.

DOWN PAYMENT UP

When you search high and low
    For a house you can buy,
You might as well know
    You'll be finding it high.

PLANT AND PULL

We always buy too many seeds,
Hope springs eternal—so do weeds.

RG SLSH BTS

She telephoned, I made a note
Abbreviating as I wrote;
Now later when I find I need it,
It's quite impossible to read it.

16

BIT OF DOGGEREL

The puppy brought his master's slippers
   (The pair that's lined with fleece)
Tightly clutched in eager nippers,
   He brought them piece by piece.

COZY, ISN'T IT?

Steam on the mirror and boats on the hamper,
The crumpled-up towels could hardly be damper;
Toothbrushes, socks, and a Donald Duck book,
Our bath simply swarms with that lived-in look.

FICKLE FICTION

About these novels called best-sellers
Whose heroines are bedroom-dwellers:
If every wife would act that way
Who'd bake the cakes for PTA?

TARDY THOUGHT

After the party I stare at debris,
(The clean-up committee is gonna be me.)
It would have been smarter to come as a guest
For now I could blithely go home with the rest.

AMNESIA

I rush upstairs at breakneck speed
To get some article I need;
But now I'm here my mind's a fuzz,
Good grief! I wonder what it was?

SWEET DREAMS

I plan all the things I'll be doing tomorrow
   While comfortably lying in bed;
However, next morning I find to my sorrow
   My muscles were all in my head.

LONG RUN

Colds, of course, eventually go;
But usually only blow by blow.

FAME IS RELATIVE

My name was once my very own,
   I married, took another;
Now usually I find I'm known
   As just the Rose kids' mother.

REPEAT ORDER

The telephone rings and the rackets begin,
The cat demands out and the dog demands in,
The kids begin fighting, the doorbell is braying;
I'm sorry, I didn't quite catch what you're saying.

MY, MY

I read what super-housewives do:
(With one hand tied behind them, too)
Raise kids, keep house, and never fag,
Head clubs, give parties, sew—and brag.

GREMLINS

My bedroom slippers, left and right,
Were neatly side by side last night;
At dawn I inched from bed and found
Somebody'd changed my feet around.

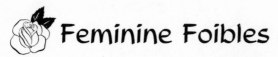 # Feminine Foibles

SISTERS UNDER THE LIPSTICK

Women in Thunderbirds airing French poodles,
Women with children in stores buying noodles,
Women in offices typing out doodles;
Fated to follow the same old plan,
Arranging their lives around some darned man.

LATE AND SOON

I can easily handle the late hours I keep
But getting up mornings is ruining my sleep.

TYRO TYPIST

Though electric typewriters are all very well,
She wishes they'd make a machine that can spell.

FELINE FRIENDS

Two neighbors became buddy-buddy I've heard,
Because they intensely detested a third.

STRIKES TO SPARE

Now bowling's become such a popular craze,
The ladies that hang around alleys these days!

BOARD MEMBER

She goes to the meeting resolved to keep still,
Her lip will be zipped, her remarks will be nil;
The session's half-done when some yakking occurs,
The voice is familiar—good heavens, it's hers!

WAIL OF A SALE

The clothes they have terrific buys in
Are never ones they have your size in.

MORPHEUS CHICKENS OUT

You're counting sheep (a silly rite)
    To woo the God of snoozing;
Then find, some long provoking night,
    The Muse just ain't a-Musing.

SI, SI

Things I should do have been piling so high
Till now they look bigger and taller than I.
I do what I can (even jobs I don't wanna)
The rest I put off and put off till manana.

HOUSE DETECTIVE

I look for hours when something's lost
And finally find where it's been tossed;
Why can't I get my search reversed
And learn to look last places first?

FAVORITE TEACHER

She loves each child but takes no sauce,
"Honey behave, or I'll be cross!"
Contented, Honey does her bidding
For Honey knows she isn't kidding.

FACING IT

Photographers are apt to carp
Unless a picture's clear and sharp;
Of late this seems a bit absurd,
A snap of me is better blurred.

GAB ON TAP

She scoops choice bits of gossip up
　　But waits awhile to spill 'em;
When holes in conversation yawn
　　She has the dirt to fill 'em.

STARDUST

I'm a square or a cube or perhaps an oblong,
I wince at the beat of a rock 'n roll song;
Pop music today simply can't hold a glove to
The magical tunes I once fell in love to.

SLOW HELLO

I phrase the letter in my mind,
It's going to be the witty kind;
It later takes the same old rut
"I meant to answer sooner, but ... "

POLLY WANNA WOG?

Consider how the froggish mamas
(Whose children all resemble commas)
Must watch not just one offspring's wriggles
But fifty thousand pollywiggles.

WEARY SHOPPER

Dresses of every conceivable kind,
    Hundreds and thousands to see;
It's truly amazing how many I find
    That look like the devil on me.

AM I A CAT!

She's read a book on rearing kids,
    Knows more than all the sages;
But judging by the one she raised
    She must have skipped some pages.

HERE LIES...

Just one more chapter, then to bed,
Just one more snack, then I'll be fed,
Just one more program to be heard,
Just one more minute, one more word;
I couldn't make a child of three
Believe the fibs I tell to me.

FIGHT, FIGHT

Teaching children how to "share"
Can be a delicate affair;
Who's the grabber? Who's abused?
Frankly, even I'm confused.

SLOW POKE

She's going out, but what to don?
Her coat, her shoes, her pearls are gone.
Her matching wardrobe's been dispersed;
Her teen-age daughters got there first.

WILL IT EVER END?

I murmur "I'll be seeing you,"
And leave someone I've chatted to;
Then grocery-carting down each aisle,
We meet and meet and smile and smile.

OPEN MEETING

I make a suggestion,
   Alas, what a pity!
My mouth's barely closed
   Till I'm on a committee.

SO I SHOULD WORRY?

"You can't take it with you," they tell me;
   The prospect is nothing I fear.
The way any salesman can sell me
   I can't even keep it while here.

BEST OF THE YEAR

Miss Cotton, Miss Pipe Stem, Miss Apricot Pie,
Miss Ankles, Miss Shape, Miss Baloney-on-Rye;
I'm waiting with awe and a sliver of dread
To see who'll be chosen as Miss Pointed Head.

OVER-PUNCTUAL

Though often late for lunch at noon
   Today I pulled a dilly;
For I arrived a week too soon
   And scared my hostess silly.

JUNIOR'S SICK

Your paper's late and I regret it;
   It wasn't even folded right.
You were lucky, though, to get it;
   Mama did the route tonight.

MISS UMMPH, MR. WHOSIS

Why is it names escape me so
When introducing friends I know?
I stand there gurgling, mouth akimbo;
My mind has packed and fled to limbo.

LIGHT BITE

My housewife mind is rather slow
Compared to lunchers in the know;
A cafeteria line's so fast
That by the time I choose, I'm past.

IT'S GOTTA GO SOMEPLACE

She pulls her belt a trifle tighter,
Sure enough, her waist looks slighter;
But her figger isn't trigger,
Something else is looking bigger.

SCHIZOPHRENIA, PERHAPS?

When doctors tell me face to face
I clearly understand my case;
Ten minutes later, like as not,
I can't recall just what I've got.

ACCENT ON U.S.A.

I like the crisp Bostonian speech,
The drawling of a Georgia Peach,
The plain, mid-western way with words,
The Bronx interpreting of "birds."
I even actually enjoy it
When people ask "You from Dee-troy-it?"

WONDER WHY?

When meeting new people, they're apt to proclaim
    I remind them of someone they know,
But nobody's yet ever mentioned the name
    Of Marilyn (Cheesecake) Monroe.

INTERMISSION

She hurried through work like a whip-driven slave,
So proud of the time she had managed to "save"
And then for some reason completely unknown,
She gabbed it all up in an hour on the phone.

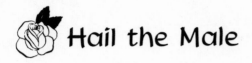 # Hail the Male

BRUTAL FACT

He used to see both far and plenty
    But now his eyes do neither;
His sight's no longer twenty-twenty
    But then he isn't either.

GONE GREEN

He notes as they're shooting the moon with his jack,
They've made no arrangements for shooting it back.

GREAT DEBATE

She loves most anything antique,
Old dishes, silver, chairs that squeak;
Her husband doesn't understand,
He thinks they're simply second-hand

NICE TRY, THOUGH

He read that if husbands would compliment wives
Such praise would enormously brighten their lives;
That evening he said, "What a pretty dress, dear."
"You crazy?" she asked him, "I've worn it a year."

QUIZ SHOW

Doctors are fine when you feel rather droopy,
But really, sometimes they're uncommonly snoopy;
They probe around jabbing with needle and gauge
And for some silly reason keep asking your age.

CLOSE CALL

His diet flipped and lost control,
  He gained two pounds last night;
His hostess set a peanut bowl
  Too near his appetite.

AFTER DINNER SPEAKERS

I would liefer
They'd be briefer.

HEAR, HEAR

A man wouldn't gossip, oh, not on your life!
He'll simply repeat what he's heard from his wife.

SUPERIOR WIT

When once he was only a guy on the staff,
He had to be clever to pull down a laugh;
But now he's the boss he has noted as how
Any old joke he relates is a wow.

HEAD OF THE HOUSE

He buys new suits occasionally,
   I coax him into that;
But winter, summer, spring and fall,
   He wears the same old hat.

SALE TALE

What's a salesman? He's the guy
Who blithely claims if he were I
He'd feel as lucky as could be
To buy the thing he's selling me!

WASTED WATTS

Men turn off lights with such a will
And save three pennies on the bill,
Then let a freezer door stand wide
Debating over snacks inside.

GUESS WHO?

From Monday to Friday he's properly clad,
A clean-shaven, gray-flannel, white-collar ad;
On Saturdays, though, he can't wait to become
A T-shirted, baggy-pants, stubble-faced bum.

FIND-IT-YOURSELF FAN

When lost, I like to ask somewhere,
My husband thinks this isn't fair;
He'll track it down—oh, he's a smarty!
Who cares we've missed two-thirds the party?

SPRING REDECORATING

When choosing paints, we stay serene;
Though I like blue, my husband green.
Each year we've both agreed, somehow;
In fact, I'm used to green by now.

SEX REFLEX

If men flock around her
    To tell her she's cute,
She finds other women
    Are apt to be mute.

SCENIC NOTE

What skill it takes for engineers
    To place the beams and ridges
Exactly so they'll hide the view
    From cars that cross the bridges.

TWO COUPLES IN A CAR

Before they are married, when taking a ride
He wants his girl cuddled up close by his side;
But after the wedding, it's yakety-yak
With men in the front and the women in back.

RUSH HOUR

By car, bus, or subway
From here-to to there-to
You meet loads of people
You don't really care to.

OUT OF FILE

She has a compulsion to keep the house "neat,"
Her husband has finally admitted defeat;
He fears, if he gets up at night for a snack,
His bed will be made if he doesn't race back.

HONE UP, HONEY

Kiss me tender,
  Kiss me brave,
But not, my love,
  Until you shave.

MAN'S WORLD

After dinner when everyone wants to collapse
Who's washing the dishes? Who's taking the naps?

DAD'S HAD IT

His family's closeknit—that's dandy, he guesses;
It's what a psychologist constantly stresses.
A thousand mile trip in a luggage packed car
And he broods, "Is togetherness carried too far?"

THE BIGGER THEY ARE...

She catches a cold but must manage to work
With children to care for and coffee to perk;
He catches a virus but can't do a lick,
It takes all his energy just being sick.

RUN-AROUND

"The population's growing fast."
    No statement could be truer.
For every time he drives a car
    The parking space is fewer.

YOU DO ALL THE WORK!

Some wives get most indignant,
  Think the boss should have a quiz,
When their husbands aren't promoted
  And some other dumb cluck is.

TOO LATE

She agreed to share his bed and board
Before she knew how loud he snored.

SILLY BOY

She wants to spend their saved-up dough
On furniture or things that show;
Her husband, who's a stubborn lout,
Insists the eaves are rusting out.

WELL, SHUT MY MOUTH

We watched as a car cut in wildly ahead;
"Some fool woman driver," my dear husband said.
We pulled up beside as the stoplight began,
And whaddya know? The fool was a man.

HASHING IT OVER

She makes a stupid play at bridge,
His frowning forehead plows a ridge
Which tells her, though he's now polite,
There'll be some pillow-chat tonight.

BROKEN PROMISE

His alibi's conceivable
But isn't quite believable.
I start to speak, then stop and sigh;
I might as well just let it lie.

YIPPEE!

The family's leaping with delight
And Mama's serving steak tonight;
They're making plans of all the ways
They'll soon be spending Daddy's raise.

CONTRACT

What's a lawyer? He's a man
Who tells you what you can't or can;
A writer of judicial jazz
Who usually begins "Whereas."

LIP SWITCH

The lipstick ads rave, "Kissable!"
"Men find it irresistible!"
Perhaps it's true, for hers is gone—
Resist or not, he's got it on.

JAW JITTERS

My dentist is deft, and his drilling is light
    Besides, he's a very fine fellow.
I never would feel one iota of fright
    Except that, quite frankly, I'm yellow.

SPECIALIST

A plumber is a man of parts,
A doctor of internal arts;
A surgeon for an ailing drain
And other matters subterrane.

IT FIGURES

What are engineers? They're sharks
Who know their angles, cubes and arcs.
They're always busy finding uses
For gimmicks like hypotenuses.

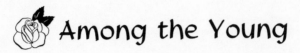 # Among the Young

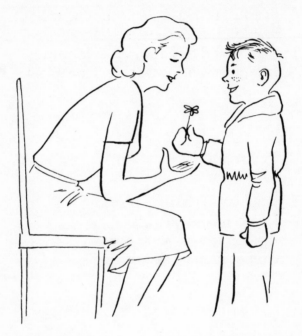

AUDIT

Sometimes I'd trade my children in
For twenty cents and think I'd win,
And then they'll grin and there am I
With riches millions couldn't buy.

GET GOING, KID!

The baby's somewhat overdue,
Two weeks ago it missed its cue;
Each day the same old words resound,
"For heaven's sake! You still around?"

OF GIFTS AND THRIFT

Baby One gets lovely things,
Baby Two gets cups and rings,
Baby Three gets shirts and gowns,
Baby Four gets hand-me-downs.

R-R-REVENGE

A baby thinks it most uncouth
How parents probe for that first tooth;
He's helpless now and thus polite
But when it's in, he's gonna bite!

DEEP STUDY

The sunlight sprawls the floor in patches
And Baby Martha raptly snatches;
What is this bright mysterious gold
She sees and feels but cannot hold?

MR. 14 MONTHS

He'll crawl under tables and push open doors,
The interesting cupboards and stairs he explores!
This world is so curious, of which he is king;
Why blame him for getting the feel of the thing?

OPEN HATCH

How toddlers love to drop toys down
A fascinating, watery john;
A tooth-brush, soap, a pinafore—
Is nothing sacred anymore?

POCKETBOOK SIZE

Sister is two and as big as a minute,
Her miniature purse doesn't have a thing in it,
While Grandma's purse bulges, excitingly wide;
A lifetime of habits are jammed up inside!

NIGHTLY QUESTION

He's sleeping, rosy-cheeked and limp,
  A cherub on display;
What happened to that little imp
  I chased around all day?

YARD-HIGH VIEW

When shopping, a child feels excessively small
While everyone else looks oppressively tall;
Mom pulls him along as she hastily hustles
And all he can see is an aisle full of bustles.

SMALL SUNDAY CALL

The doorbell rings out with a company sound,
I swoop up the newspapers scattered around,
Slip shoes on my feet and some lipstick on me,
Fling open the door—to a neighbor, aged three.

PLAYBACK

She listens to her daughter Kay
  Who's bossing dolls around;
And wonders with surprised dismay,
  "Is *that* the way I sound?"

MAN AND BOY

He gingerly mounted a thirty-foot ladder,
    Then suddenly felt rather gone;
His 4-year-old son had come gayly behind him
    And *he* had his roller-skates on!

KINDERGARTEN ART

He proudly brings his painting home;
A horse? A dog? A tree? A gnome?
He gets provoked at dumb old me,
It's Daddy, any fool can see!

THERE, THERE, HONEY

Susan is miserable rather than sick;
I cut all her fingernails down to the quick
And bathe her to quiet the worst of the sting:
Chicken pox (scratch) is an itch-of-a-thing.

ITCHING PALM

Most everyone's hand
    Instinctively spreads
To swish across little boys'
    Brush-cut heads.

MORNING SCRAMBLE

Where's Sonny's belt, his other sock,
His gloves, his books, his pen, his lock?
He's finally off, Mom's set to fold;
Then finds her coffee's dank and cold.

TRUMPET AND LUMP IT

Junior begged us for a horn,
   Those strident notes are his,
He wouldn't practice, we'd have sworn;
   Unfortunately he is.

WILL SHE, WON'T SHE?

Piano practice zips along
Till Sister hits a note that's wrong;
A pause ensues—ears cringe a mite
Until (oh joy!) she hits it right.

CRISIS EVERY WEEK

Six stitches are in where he fell on his chin,
   He's bandaged but not even fazed;
He flips me a grin but I'm frankly all in.
   Is this how a boy must be raised?

LIPSTICK

Girls are old enough to wear it
  (At least, so I would judge)
Before the boys are old enough
  To know what makes it smudge.

THAT'S MY BOY!

A daughter's sweet, a daughter's nice,
But when there's snow and when there's ice,
And when there's shoveling to be done,
How lovely is a muscled son!

MORE POWER TO HER

He cleaned up his nails with no nagging by me,
  He changed to some freshly-pressed pants;
Apparently Junior fell madly in love
  At the Friday night Junior High dance.

BROWNIES

Beanie hats and "smiles in pockets,"
Energies that flare like rockets;
Packaged in a thousand wriggles,
Brownies come complete with giggles.

SALUTE TO GIRL SCOUTS

"On my honor, I will try . . ."
What wondrous words to grow up by!

CUB SCOUTS

Not a thing in the world can demolish her poise
If she's been a Den Mother to six or eight boys.

TO BOY SCOUT LEADERS

Because you take the time to care,
And somehow make the time to spare,
The Scouting creed, in whole or parts,
Forever lives in boyish hearts.

TENTATIVE TEEN

The teenager world has a special design,
Bounded by school and a telephone line;
It has its own worries and coins its own jokes
And feeds upon hamburgers, pizza, and cokes.

INNER CIRCLE

They say she's too young to be late on a date,
Too old for the teasing and tantrums of eight;
It's hard to be only betwixt and between
At the wonderful, miserable age of thirteen.

LOST SOPRANO

Every few days I get one of these scares,
I hear a man's voice in a bedroom upstairs;
And then I remember (with slightly red face)
My son, who's 13, has just shifted to bass.

FAST AGING

They painted the nursery not too long ago,
For years the same colors seemed most apropos;
But now it all needs a complete decorating,
The woodwork's the same—but Baby is dating.

ALL NIGHT GIGGLE

What a blast a pajama-clad party can be,
With pizza at midnight and brownies at three.
It's not until five that the girls settle down;
"Next time," mutters Father, "I'll be out of town."

MEMO TO ADULTS

"You've grown!" they gasp, as if astonished;
And Stuart stands as if admonished,
But wonders through the pause ensuing
Just what they figured he'd be doing?

PREVIEW OF PROM DRESS

She's trying it on for her Dad, who's declaring
He personally thinks it's a trifle too daring;
He's smiling inside as he's saying it, though,
At her loafers and bobby socks showing below.

JUNIOR'S NEW RECORD

I'm glassy-eyed, my fingers twitch,
My thoughts are pied, my ear-drums itch;
He's played it for the sixteenth time,
He isn't tired of it, but I'm.

NEW BOY-FRIEND

He enters the living room, suddenly shy;
Her family's assembled to give him the eye.
The friendly once-over may seem a bit stiff
When even the dog ambles over to sniff.

MEMO TO AVERAGE GIRL

You see a girl that's prettier,
Don't envy her but pity her;
When years go by, as years will do,
She has more looks to lose than you!

GOBBLE-DE-GOOK

Our teenager, Doug, is perpetually hollow;
It's hard to believe the amounts he can swallow.
Those in-between snacks he'll so casually fix
Use up what I'd planned as a supper for six.

GROWING UP

You think as kids increase in age
Sometime they'll reach an easy stage;
You later wish for time's reverse
Because the stage that's next is worse.

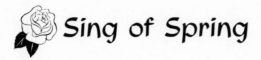 # Sing of Spring

BUSY LIFE

The yeast of spring is doubling up
And crocus blooms come bubbling up;
Forsythia's knitting golden mittens
And pussy willow pops her kittens.

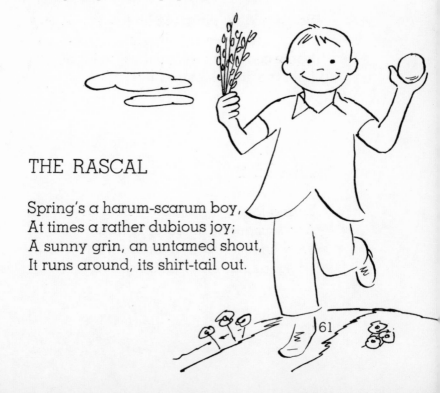

THE RASCAL

Spring's a harum-scarum boy,
At times a rather dubious joy;
A sunny grin, an untamed shout,
It runs around, its shirt-tail out.

61

APRIL FOOL, MOM!

They plan their tricks and play their parts,
And, bless their corny little hearts,
They have at hand the perfect dupe;
I'm such an unsuspecting stupe.

SPRINGTIME FIRSTS

Some people plant the first sweet peas,
Some take an early dip and freeze;
Some see the first wee wren in flight,
I get the first mosquito bite.

FRAGILE

Young love's a rootless, tender thing
As transient as an early spring;
Why smash it with a jocose word?
I'd sooner club a humming bird.

EASTER PARADE

Junior has a brand-new suit,
Sister has a coat that's cute;
Mother has a hat and dress,
Father has a clean-and-press.

THOUGHTFUL GIFT

My youngest son, who's creature-smitten,
For Easter gave his Mom a kitten;
Although somewhat surprised, of course,
I'm *so* relieved it's not a horse.

SHELL GAME

The Easter eggs this year were smashed;
The Easter bunny had them stashed
In Daddy's chair beneath the pad,
And no-one thought of warning Dad.

SPORTS WIDOW

Whenever bowling season ends
    She does some wistful wishing,
That maybe he'll stay home again.
    (He'll switch to golf or fishing.)

GOLF IS SO SAD

He hardly can wait for his very first shot,
This year he'll break ninety as likely as not;
He tees up correctly, his left arm is stiff,
As he belts out a truly magnificent whiff.

APRIL FASHION NOTE

Boys are bursting at the seams,
Trousers tight across the beams,
Buttons pop and cuffs ride high;
Mama's gonna have to buy.

MASS RECOVERY

Though half of the staff
    Has been out with the flu,
They all report back
    When a payday is due.

ADIOS,
INCOME TAX DOLLARS

I could have learned to love you so,
But now, too soon, you have to go;
Together we'd have had such fun,
But you've been called to Washington.

AFTER SCHOOL

My darlings come home with a "Hi" and a thud,
Their heads full of dreams, their feet full of mud.

CRASH NO. 17

I shudder whenever a baseball is thrown:
Our garage has a window that's accident prone.

WATCH YOUR DIET, FISH

Anglers always have an angle,
Some new bait or flashy spangle;
Nibble slyly, nibble sparsely,
Or you'll wear a sprig of parsley.

SMALL-TOWN MEMORY

The river looped a mile away,
I'd wander down a springtime day
To woods where clumps of violets grew;
None since have blossomed quite so blue.

MOTHER OF THE YEAR

Mothers come all shapes and sizes
In a thousand different guises;
Is there one who's really best
Above the loving, faithful rest?

If each daughter and each son
Could cast a vote for only one,
It would instantly be known
The perfect Mother is our own.

'TEN-SHUN!

The tulips form a line of march,
Their posture trim and prim as starch;
Their colors flash hip-hip-hooray,
Parading down the streets of May.

TWO GIRLS OF TEN
(Memorial Day)

BORN 1802, the gravestone said;
DIED 1812, young Betsy read.
"Nobody left," she thought, "to care,"
And laid three rosebuds gently there.

MISS 16

A girl gets a bid to a glamorous dance,
Immediately problems arise of finance;
A dreamy new dress, will the old slippers do?
If boys only knew what a budget goes through!

MR. 16

A boy bids a girl to a glamorous dance,
Arrives with a car and a crease in his pants;
Tickets, corsage, and the gas he must buy,
If girls only knew what a date costs a guy!

CAP AND GOWN

The tests and corny classroom jokes,
The pizza, dances, games, and Cokes;
The paper, chalk, and book aroma
All wrapped up in this diploma.

QUITE A START

What costly wedding gifts they show
Compared to twenty years ago!
Some presents modern brides will get
Their mothers haven't even yet.

DAWN YAWN

The dew is busy shining grass,
The starlings chirp alert, en masse,
The sun's a brisk and flaming red;
I wish that I were back in bed.

CHUCK-HOLE LANE

I bounce with mounting apprehensions,
    I fear the axle's bent;
They paved the road with good intentions,
    They should have used cement.

HOMING INSTINCT

Now take a pair of boyish feet:
They'll gravely plow a puddled street,
Then squish up steps and through the door
To drip-dry on the kitchen floor.

Strum of Summer

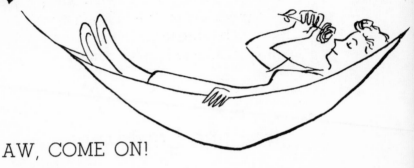

AW, COME ON!

Forget the world and problems in it;
  Roses sing a scented tune,
So rest your head for just a minute
  In the lazy lap of June.

DEARLY BELOVED

The bride is white narcissus lace,
A string of pearls, a tender face;
Of all the people in the room
She's the one who sees the groom.

NAME-TAPES

She's gotta sew 'em on their clothes
   Or press 'em on like little stamps;
It would be simpler, heaven knows,
   If kids attended nudist camps.

OUTBOUND OUTBOARDS

Roads are packed with cars and trailers,
Towing boats for week-end sailors;
Two hundred miles without a break
To putt-putt three across a lake.

MIDDLE-WEIGHT

The kids outgrow their bathing suits,
   The new ones I must buy!
But as I tug my old one on,
   What's sadder—so have I.

2 GALLONS, PLEASE

Little children have to go,
They're never timed together though;
So parents, driving on vacations,
Spend half their time at filling stations.

WIDE EXPANSE

He knows that her chassis is curvingly classy,
    Her face is appealingly dear;
But begging her pardon, while weeding the garden,
    The view is unfortunately rear.

NEVER CAN TELL

In music and sports, in books and resorts,
    Their tastes coincided all right,
However, romance muffed a beautiful chance;
    They detested each other on sight.

INCLUDING SHOES

Our travelling bags are neatly packed
    And I'd be feeling deft
Except for this unhappy fact:
    Three piles of stuff are left.

TRANSIENT NEIGHBORS

On our left a noisy crew
Keep banging doors till nearly two;
On our right folks rise at dawn,
Thirty minutes till they're gone.
Motel life has little tedium,
Try to sleep a happy medium!

VACATION TRIP

Before a family hits the road
Mom washes, irons, and packs the load;
Dad helps, of course, as you'd expect:
He takes the car to have it checked.

LOOKIT!

We can't go far until we're halted
To buy a hamburg or a malted;
Our kids, who miss the scenery,
Spot every roadside beanery.

FISH-MATES

He's perfectly willing to hook 'em,
She's perfectly willing to cook 'em;
However, a problem still rises between 'em
For neither is perfectly willing to clean 'em.

LITTLE GIRL AT PICNIC

She fell in the tub that was cooling the pop,
She wrestled the ketchup until it went plop,
She kept both her parents on jittery toes
And managed to use up three changes of clothes.

STYLE NOTE

As the weather waxes hotter
People's inhibitions totter
And women do their shopping shorted
In shapes surprisingly assorted.

TO A 20-INCH FAN

My craze for you will doubtless pall
And quickly cool by early fall.
But now you've won my heart with ease;
I love the way you shoot the breeze.

NOT SWAT

How clever of the fly to buzz
Not where it is but where it was.

ON TAP

They took a camping trip out West
Which Mom enjoyed with all the rest;
Except, occasionally, she'd think
How lovely is a kitchen sink!

OFFICE ONCE-OVER

Back from vacation?
  They stare at your pan
And measure your fun
  By the depth of your tan.

KIN DROP INN

Up to your cottage loaded for fair
To find that your in-laws are already there.

JUST IN CASE

We shop in air-conditioned stores
Then sun outside and fry our pores;
In after life we'll thus be sure
To weather either temperature.

TOE-TEMPTING

Although the plastic bathing pool
Was bought to keep the children cool
It's odd how often they compete
With several pairs of grown-up feet.

78

ZOO FAN

I want to see tigers, the baby giraffe,
The peacocks, the deer, and the buffalo calf;
I want to ride trains, see the chimps in a show,
Try pitching some peanuts to bears in the know.
How nice I have children to use as excuses,
For Mama just loves seeing monkeys and mooses.

HOT SEAT

Skirts can stick to chairs
    And do,
But when you're wearing shorts
    It's you.

FEEDIN' COUSINS

People who travel on budget vacations
Artfully plan it around their relations.

LADY, BE COOL

The evening's hot and heavy
　Where the streaks of sun have lain;
I wish tonight would make her bed
　With silver sheets of rain.

TEMPERED TONE

With windows open in the summer
Folks should certainly be mummer;
Keep their voices soft and cheerful
Or the neighbors get an earful.

AUGUST GARDEN PARTY

A little loud, a little flashy,
Their debut is bright and splashy;
While cultured flowers are looking droopy
Marigolds are making whoopee!

CLEAN SWEEP

Little drops of water, little grains of sand,
May make the mighty ocean and the mighty land,
    But puddled on a cottage floor
      They're apt to make a mother sore.

GUEST HOUSE

Last month they entertained her kin,
She gaily fed and roomed them in;
This month she's frazzled to a friz,
The visiting relatives are his.

HORS D'OEUVRE

Out-door barbecues, I fear,
  Have one unhappy flaw;
While waiting for the steaks to sear
  Mosquitoes eat *me* raw.

HAY FEVER HOPE

Pollen, stay deep in the heart of a posy;
Sniffing at me, you're insufferably nosy.

ALICE? ANN? ART?

It drives me nuts when postcards come
And I can't figure who they're from;
Of all my friends initialed A
Who the heck's in Monterey?

WHO'S FOR CRIBBAGE?

Don't ask me for tennis,
That back-handed menace,
My smashes dissolve into lobs;
A go at croquet
Simply ruins my day,
I miss all the thing-a-ma-bobs.

A sailboat is fine
But thanks, I'll decline,
I'm aft when I should have been fore;
Though golf has its charm
Quit twisting my arm,
I can't even lie a good score.

I get me the birds
In some very short words
When I whiff on a badminton court;
I try but I goof
With monotonous proof
That I'm only a Spectator Sport.

I *like* flabby muscles
And pallid corpuscles,
I crave no athletic renown;
I'm frightfully game
And a lovable dame,
If only you'd let me sit down!

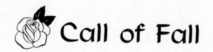 # Call of Fall

REVEILLE

Vacation is over and back to the nest,
How smugly you murmur that home is the best.
Next day as alarms buzz you out of the sack
You wonder why anyone ever comes back.

GET SET!

He's ready for teachers,
    He's bubbling with vim;
My question is whether
    They're ready for him.

GONE TO WAIST

Strawberry sundaes and summertime snacks,
Cokes and potato chips, hamburgs in stacks;
Shopping for dresses this autumn, it's clear
They're making size 12 a lot smaller this year.

NOT YET FIVE

He haunts the front steps, lost and lonely;
Of all his gang, the one and only
Who's not allowed to start to school.
Some silly, stupid, grown-up rule!

SLIVER OF ENVY

September's poignant, golden haze
Recalls absorbing campus days;
I watch collegiate dolls and guys
With wistful, green-as-ivy eyes.

NEXT YEAR, DEAR

Please fish for committees in some fresher pool
Of mothers with children just starting to school.
Quite frankly I've had it, my pep is played out;
After eight solid years I'm all PTA'd out.

SMIRK, SMIRK

The people I know who look smuggest of all
Are ones who have saved their vacations till fall.

DETROIT VIRUS

He's caught a disease that is going around
And all that will cure it is money, he's found;
Whenever he passes a showroom he'll twitch,
He's got what is known as the "new-model" itch.

NO DOUGH, NO GO

Fall has arrived when the letters come in
From organizations about to begin;
Somewhere between the announcements and news
Is the delicate hint to be snappy with dues.

1, 2, 3, 4,--5?

Time has fled beyond recall,
The baby started school this fall;
A fleeting thought keeps nagging Mother,
Should she maybe have another?

AMO, AMAS, AMAT

She once was such a Latin whiz
She thought she'd help her son with his;
How shocked she was to find instead
The language is, indeed, quite dead.

COLLEGIATE MIGRATION

Now it's back to Minnesota, Notre Dame and OSU,
To U of M, the Ivy League, to Hillsdale and Purdue;
Each fall I envy college men,
They'll never know so much again!

YEA, SPORT!

What thrills attend a football game!
What passes, punts, what wild acclaim!
How strong the line! The backs—how fleet!
How loud the cheers! How c-c-cold my feet.

TV BIZ

He spends his time each Saturday
    At watching football scenes;
And that is why, quite sad to say,
    Our windows still have screens.

NATURE NOTE

The geese form a confident V in the sky,
Instinctively flying as straight as a die;
While people go tacking from wisdom to folly,
Living their lives by guess and by golly.

FALL PAL

She's busy all year taking care of their setter,
Her husband is only too anxious to let her;
The season for pheasant will open—yea men!
And all of a sudden it's *his* dog again.

TRICKY TREAT

They feel so rich with all their loot,
The suckers, candy bars, and fruit;
Till Mama puts it all away
To dole it out a piece a day.

FALL MATRON

Her suit is of worsted, her hat fluffs a veil,
Her furpiece keeps endlessly biting its tail.

HOMECOMING

"Come back," your Alma Mater calls,
"And see my brand-new labs and halls,
My brand-new dorm with penthouse deck;
Come back and bring a brand-new check."

BUCKING THE ODDS

Intrepid hunters venture forth
To track and tramp the frozen north;
What gallant sports! But just the same,
The deer's the one that's really game.

TURKEY TALK

White meat or dark meat,
    Drumstick or breast,
The guests have their choice
    And to hash with the rest.

HALF THE FUN

I rarely shop for Christmas early
Though later it's a hurly-burly;
My spirit's rather non-committal
Till people start to hint a little.

 # Yoicks! Winter

CHRISTMAS PLAY

In angel robes he looked divine,
It didn't seem he could be mine
Until his halo slipped, and then
I recognized my son again.

OUR FOREFATHERS

No cars, no phones, no cheese with chives,
But still they led quite happy lives;
What puzzles me and makes me gape
Is how they lived without Scotch Tape.

POLITE PLIGHT

At parties she makes an exception on diet;
She eats what the hostess provides and is quiet.
But holiday dinners are ruining her schemes;
Too many exceptions are splitting her seams.

DELIVER ME!

Some women look so chic and proper,
But I'm a take-it-with-me shopper.
I just can't wait to have stuff sent;
The worse I look, the more I've spent.

DECEMBER BIRTHDAY

Don't expect any gifts if your birthday's before,
You'll get 'em on Christmas (supposedly more)
Your birthday comes after, dear sir or dear madam?
Expecting some presents? Why honey, you've had 'em!

LUXURY AD

"Who buys such gifts?" I gasp, aghast.
For "little" things the price seems vast;
A fifty dollar handkerchief?
A person wouldn't *dare* to sniff!

WHO IN THE WORLD?

We met a Mister Brown last fall
But never knew his wife at all;
We won't find out till late in May
They sent the card signed "Jean and Ray."

OUTSIDE DECORATIONS

Some windows are vivid with painted-on scenes,
Some doorways are lighted and gala with greens;
I vow each December I'll surely do more,
Then all I get up is a wreath on the door.

HOLIDAY WHIRL

The revolving door races around in a spin,
My arms full of bundles I'm scared to leap in.

THOSE LUCKY PEOPLE!

The stars press their noses on panes of the sky
And watch with a wistful and wondering eye,
As parents bring gifts from a hideaway place
To answer the dreams on a child's sleeping face.

BIG DECISION

A crimson tie caught Miss Five's eye,
Just right for Dad but priced too high;
Her problem charms the crowded store,
Is Daddy worth a quarter more?

LAST MINUTE FLURRY

As snow drifts down in twinkling flight
They're sweeping out the skies tonight;
The housewives of the Milky Way
Are dusting stars for Christmas Day.

CHRISTMAS SHOPPER, JR.

He scans the counter, serious eyed,
And stands on tiptoe to decide.
It's up to him to choose the best,
More splendid, far, than all the rest;
As, watched by smiling dime-store girls,
He buys his Mom a string of pearls.

CHECKER-UPPER

Grandma's gift took lots of thought,
She has to use what Junior bought;
So if you're wondering how come,
That's why she's chewing bubble gum.

SAFE DISTANCE

It wasn't Dad, it wasn't Mum
Who paid the cash for Sister's drum,
But relatives in Santa Fe
At least a thousand miles away.

GIFT OF TRUTH

Junior's thank-you notes are short,
His letters aren't the gabby sort;
"The shirt is fine but kind of loose
Thanks anyway—yours Truly, Bruce."

SCHOOL'S OUT, YULE'S IN

Children wait with such elation
Counting days till this vacation;
Mama's busy keeping track
Counting days till they go back.

BABY NEW YEAR

Bless its brand-new little heart,
It looks so cunning at the start;
But well I know, before it's through,
This one will run me ragged, too.

OWE AND OW

Charge accounts were sweet as pie
Inviting us to buy, buy, buy,
Until the bills came in today
Inviting us to pay, pay, pay.

RESOLUTION

I resolve to be calm with the kids about things;
My patience will sprout me a halo and wings.
A crash interrupts me before I've begun,
"For heaven's sake, Junior, *now* what have you done?"

BOOT JOCKEY

Galoshes and snowsuits, then out the kids go
But quickly return with five neighbors in tow;
They're inside for thawing and outside to play
Till Mama's whole morning is zippered away.

SNOW BUNNIES

Some girls will go skiing
   Because they like skiis,
While others go only
   To meet all the he's.

PARTY STREET

"We'll leave the porch light on," they said,
I'm sure they did for up ahead
Each house is lit right down the line;
The question is, which host is mine?

HOMEMADE VALENTINE

He'll bring her lovely flowers, perhaps,
Or chocolate creams in fancy wraps;
But if he *does* forget, she wishes,
He'd be a sport and do the dishes.

COMPARATIVE COMFORT

I read about the London fogs
And California's choking smogs,
Then feel a trifle smug, I fear,
About the lousy weather here.

COLORFUL FANCY

Hope is the yeast that keeps life on the rise,
Hope is a seed catalogue in disguise;
The garden I'm planning may never bouquet,
But who wants a sensible dream anyway?

MITTEN WEATHER

Kitty doesn't like the snows,
   She doesn't like the thaws;
She stops with every step she goes
   And shakes resentful paws.

Too Late to Classify

REMEMBER, YOU ASKED

I vow in the future I'll never complain;
How lightly I'll shrug off an ache or a pain,
How nobly I'll keep my remarks at high level,
But right at the moment I feel like the devil.

LOVER LANGUAGE

What easy lines a flatterer has,
"You're wonderful," and all that jazz;
They may not seem precisely true
Unless, of course, they're said to you.

LAW OF GRAVITY

People who live it up all over town
May later have trouble in living it down.

NEW DAUGHTER-IN-LAW

She had no daughters—not a one,
Each child turned out to be a son;
But now she has, and loves to praise her;
What's more, she didn't have to raise her!

SWEET STUFF

Compliments are lovely deals,
    They make you want to chirrup;
You know just how a pancake feels
    When someone pours the syrup.

HAND-OUT

I like supporting Uncle Sam;
I'm fond of him, I truly am.
I'm sure he's careful how he spends
But man, he has expensive friends!

LOOKING AHEAD

I'd like to be a Grandma (or a Grandpa if I could);
I'd spoil somebody else's children positively good,
Then blithely turn 'em back to mama
And take a plane to Yokohama.

IS SHE IN STITCHES!

She wouldn't make her friends distraught
Discussing surgery, she thought;
And so they ring her bed in pairs,
Ignoring hers, describing theirs.

SLOW BREAK

My view on the language of TV is dim,
    The announcer and I don't agree;
What's "station identification" to him
    Are seven commercials to me.

BLAND BLEND

She works to plan a soothing diet
To keep her husband's ulcers quiet;
No coffee, tea, or coke for chow;
Thank heavens for the placid cow!

LONG AND SHORT OF IT

Some days creep by in snailing gears,
    The hours, slow-footed, chime;
But ah, the fleet quicksilver years
    Dance by in double-time.

THIN EDGE

You're always served potato chips
To dunk in cheeses whipped for dips;
They crack beneath your eager thumb
And leave you hanging by a crumb.

SNIP AND TUCK

Doctors say the surgery's simple,
   Their voices smooth as salve,
But "minor operations"
   Are what *other* people have.

CRICK IN THE--OUCH!

My neck has always been a base
That turned or kept my head in place;
Tonight it's lost its usual knack,
It swivels, but I don't come back.

PERFECT MATCH

Why'd she marry *him,* you wonder?
Seems to you she made a blunder,
While other people will aver
They're stunned by what he saw in *her.*

NOISE AND NERVES

They love every grandchild, adorably cunning,
Constantly active and asking and running;
But after a while, as they tend and caress 'em,
Grandma and Grandpa have had it—God bless 'em!

LIBRARY FINES

I take out a dozen, forget to renew;
How startled I am when they're weeks overdue.
My money's aghast at the way I can fritter it,
I'd doubtless be solvent if I were illiterate.

MAILBOX AT CORNER

I post my mail then bang the slot
So see if it has stuck or not;
This is a curious habit, as
So far no letter ever has.

BEAT FEET

The party's immense,
   It's a stand-up affair;
If I had any sense
   I'd have brought my own chair.

TIED UP

Your telephone's always obligingly ready,
That is, till your teenager starts going steady.

INSIDE DOPE

While downing get-well pills last week
I swear I heard my innards shriek,
"Man the lifeboats! Stand by, men!
Here comes a miracle pill again."

VOICE OF EXPERIENCE

Turn backward, turn backward, oh time in thy run;
For now I can see how it should have been done.

ANNIVERSARY

I promised when I said "I do"
To love and honor, cherish you;
Although such vows run long and deep
You've made them easy ones to keep.

NO FAIR

Why bad habits come so easily
    I've never understood,
When I work so hard establishing
    Just one of them that's good.

RECOMPENSE

Memories soften sorrow,
    Life has a curious way
Of paying off tomorrow
    In the coins of yesterday.

CHEWING THE CUD

When cows get together for chats do they mutter,
Comparing the prices of silage and butter?
Or do they bewail, as they noddingly graze,
How green was the grass in the good old days!

WELL, ANYWAY

We know some folks who hop a plane
And blithely fly to France or Spain;
Though stuck at home to lag about,
What flossy friends we brag about!

WITH ALL DUE CREDIT

It's normally easy to do something kind,
What's harder is putting it out of your mind;
It's tempting to brag just a little instead
And twirl a small halo on top of your head.

POOR CONVERSATIONALIST

They tell me money talks and so
  I guess mine must be shy;
It barely nods a brief hello
  Before it waves goodbye.

WATCH THOSE FIGURES!

They're always counting calories
In candy, cakes, and pies and cheese;
It's hard for people on a diet
To keep their mathematics quiet.

REVISED ESTIMATE

If every life's an open book,
  According to the sages,
I rather think we all would like
  To edit several pages.